W9-CEU-511

AMERICAN GENERALS OF WORLD WAR II

Collective Biographies

AMERICAN
GENERALS
OF
WORLD WAR II

Ron Knapp

Enslow Publishers, Inc.

44 Fadem Road	PO Box 38
Box 699	Aldershot
Springfield, NJ 07081	Hants GU12 6BP
USA	UK

Library of Congress Cataloging–in–Publication Data

Knapp, Ron.
    American generals of World War II / Ron Knapp.
        p. cm. — (Collective biographies)
    Includes bibliographical references and index.
    Summary: Profiles ten of America's greatest generals of World War II,
including Henry Arnold, Omar Bradley, Dwight D. Eisenhower,
Curtis LeMay, and Douglas MacArthur.
    ISBN 0–7660–1024–4
    1. World War, 1939–1945—Biography—Juvenile literature.
    2. Generals—United States—Biography—Juvenile literature.
    3. United States. Army—Biography—Juvenile literature. [1. World
War, 1939–1945—Biography. 2. Generals.] I. Title. II. Series.
    D736.K63   1998
    940.54'273'0922—dc21
    [B]   97–29405
                                                CIP
                                              AC

Printed in the United States of America

10 9 8 7 6 5 4 3 2 1

Photo Credits: FDR Library, pp. 11, 23, 72; Library of Congress, pp. 52,
86, 96, 104; National Archives, pp. 16, 26, 34, 48, 91, 101, 111; Patton
Museum, pp. 8, 45, 76, 82; Stock Montage, Inc., pp. 58, 68; U.S.
Army–Courtesy Harry S Truman Library, p. 65.

Cover Photo: National Archives

Contents

Preface

It was the biggest, bloodiest war in history. Almost every nation in the world was involved in World War II. Major battles were fought on three continents—Asia, Europe, and Africa. Around 17 million combatants died as a result of the war. At least that many civilians lost their lives, too.

In the 1930s three nations, Japan, Italy, and Germany, wanted more land. In order to get it, they put together powerful, well-equipped armed forces. Many of the world's other countries, still weary from World War I, which ended in 1918, were not anxious to fight—or even to develop strong armed forces of their own.

The three territory-hungry nations, which became known as the Axis Powers, started their conquests by attacking weaker, adjacent countries. In 1931, Japan began seizing parts of China. In 1935 Italy attacked Ethiopia in Africa. Without a fight, Germany took over Austria in 1938.

German leader Adolf Hitler then demanded the Sudetenland, a region of Czechoslovakia. French and British leaders believed they could prevent war by allowing him to take it. But Hitler wasn't satisfied for

The devastation caused by World War II was tremendous. Millions of soldiers and civilians lost their lives, and many more lost homes and property.

long. In 1939 he seized all of Czechoslovakia. It wasn't until German troops invaded Poland on September 1, 1939, that France and Great Britain finally declared war on Germany and its ally, Italy.

For a while, the Germans looked unstoppable. By May 1940 they had overrun Denmark, Norway, Belgium, Luxembourg, the Netherlands, and France. In Europe, Great Britain stood alone against Hitler.

In the early stages of the war, the Union of Soviet Socialist Republics (U.S.S.R.) allied itself with Germany. Also hungry for new territory, the U.S.S.R. split Poland with Germany, then captured Finland, Estonia, Latvia, and Lithuania. On June 22, 1941, Hitler turned on his old ally and sent troops into the U.S.S.R.

At this point, the United States of America was still not actively involved in the war, but, under the leadership of President Franklin D. Roosevelt, the nation leased billions of dollars worth of supplies to the nations fighting against the Axis Powers.

In 1940 Japanese troops took over Indochina. General Hideki Tojo, Japan's premier, believed that only the United States could stop his nation from controlling Asia. To keep the United States from interfering, Tojo ordered a surprise attack on the American base at Pearl Harbor, Hawaii, on December 7, 1941.

Immediately the United States entered the war against Japan. Three days later, Germany and Italy declared war on the United States. Now there were three Allies, Great Britain, the United States and the U.S.S.R., standing against the Axis Powers.

General George C. Marshall, the Army Chief of Staff, developed a battle plan for American forces. United States troops and supplies would be concentrated in the effort to help Great Britain and the U.S.S.R. defeat Germany and Italy in Africa and Europe. Only then would the Allies turn their full attention to the Japanese.

Early in the war, the Allies were having a tough time in the Pacific. Japanese troops forced General Douglas MacArthur out of the Philippines. General Joseph Stilwell and a small band of men had to escape from Burma into India.

Under the leadership of Generals Dwight D. Eisenhower, George S. Patton, and Omar N. Bradley, American troops first faced combat in North Africa. After defeating the Germans there, they landed on the Italian island of Sicily. Soon Italian dictator Benito Mussolini was forced from power and Italy surrendered.

The Germans continued fighting in Italy, but they were being pushed back on the eastern front by the U.S.S.R. Then on D-day, June 6, 1944, in the largest Allied operation of the war, American, British, and Canadian troops under Eisenhower's direction, invaded occupied France. Patton, Ridgway, and Bradley led their troops through France into Germany. Generals Henry H. Arnold and Curtis E. LeMay commanded the intensive bombing of

The United States, Great Britain, and the Union of Soviet Socialist Republics (U.S.S.R.) allied to fight the Axis powers. Here, Winston Churchill, prime minister of Great Britain, Franklin D. Roosevelt, president of the United States, and Joseph Stalin, leader of the U.S.S.R., meet at Yalta in February 1945 to discuss war plans.

German cities. In the spring of 1945, Hitler committed suicide and Germany surrendered.

Meanwhile, in the Pacific, Stilwell's men retook Burma. General Holland M. Smith's Marines captured island after island from the Japanese. As he had promised, MacArthur returned to the Philippines.

After atomic bombs were dropped on Hiroshima and Nagasaki, Japan officially surrendered on September 2, 1945. World War II was over.

The ten generals in this book were all career soldiers. Seven of them graduated from the United States Military Academy in West Point, New York. Seven of them served in the Army, two in what was then the Army's Air Force, and one in the Marines. During their careers, they were sometimes criticized for their tactics—and even for their dress. Patton was twice removed from command because of harsh comments he made about hospitalized soldiers and America's former Russian allies. The same thing happened to MacArthur when he disregarded orders during the Korean War.

These generals survived the war. Several of them held important positions after the war ended. Marshall served as secretary of state. MacArthur ruled Japan for five years. LeMay set up the Strategic Air Command, then ran for vice president. Eisenhower was elected to two terms as president.

These generals were the men who coordinated and led the American effort in World War II. As Commander in Chief, President Roosevelt, and later

President Harry S Truman, listened to their advice as they made the major strategic decisions. But the day-to-day battlefield plans, of course, had to be made by Marshall in Washington, D.C., and the other generals in combat around the world.

These generals directed the efforts that defeated Hitler, Tojo, and Mussolini in World War II. To a large degree, they are responsible for America's victory in the most costly, horrendous conflict ever fought on this planet.

Henry H. Arnold

(1886–1950)

When Henry Harley Arnold was born in Glandwyne, Pennsylvania, on June 25, 1886, there was no such thing as an airplane. The automobile was still being developed. If it was too far to walk, Americans got where they were going by riding trains, horses, carriages, or stagecoaches. The most exciting, prestigious job in the Army was to charge into battle on a horse as part of the cavalry.

When Arnold attended West Point, that was his goal. "It was the last romantic thing left on earth," he explained. "The galloping charge! Indian fighting!"[1] In fact, while he was studying to be an officer, he spent almost as much time riding horses as he did studying for classes. One of his other interests was carrying out the work of the Black Hand, a secret

General Henry H. Arnold

group of cadets dedicated to sneaking fireworks into the Academy. Arnold thoroughly enjoyed his years at West Point. His classmates even nicknamed him "Hap", because he always seemed to be smiling. He was not one of the chosen few who became cavalry officers, probably because of his low grades. Instead, in 1907 he was assigned to the Philippine Islands as an infantry officer. Leading foot soldiers through the jungle was not Arnold's idea of an Army career. He thought of resigning his commission and starting another career as a civilian, but he finally decided to go to the Philippines.

Two years later the young officer returned to the United States by way of Europe. While he was in Paris he saw his first airplane. It was a small, rickety craft in which Louis Blériot had made the first flight across the English Channel, the stretch of water that separates Great Britain from France. Flying seemed like an exciting adventure to Arnold; it was certainly better than being a foot soldier.

But at that time the United States Army had no airplanes, and Arnold was sent to Governors Island, New York, for two more years in the infantry. Once in New York, he met Wilbur Wright, who, with his brother Orville, had invented the airplane in 1903. A few months later, Arnold joined most of the early flying pioneers at the country's first international "air meet" at Belmont Park, New York. He spent hours talking with the pilots and looking over their aircraft.

By then, he had no doubt that he wanted to be a pilot, too.

Arnold got his chance in 1911. The United States decided that the plane would be an effective weapon in war, so the Army began to develop an air force. It was a dangerous job because flying was such a new science, and many of the planes crashed. Arnold was one of the first volunteers at Simms Station in Dayton, Ohio. Later it would become Huffman Field, but in 1911 it was just an unplowed cow pasture. Flying the early planes was so dangerous that a mortician's wagon, loaded with caskets, was occasionally parked next to the field.

The first military planes, built by the Wright brothers, could carry just two men for about an hour at speeds of around 40 miles per hour. The Wrights trained the pilots. For his lessons, Arnold climbed into a plane perched on sawhorses in the back of the Wrights' shop in Dayton. Flying was not a complicated business; after a few hours, he knew everything they did. When he finished training, he was America's third military pilot.

But flying was still an exciting new adventure. It was not unusual for thousands of people to gather to watch a plane land or take off. They viewed the pilots as daring young heroes who risked their lives. There were not even any seats for the pilots; they just sat on the wings. When one man fell off his plane, a decision was made to equip the rest with the first seat belts. Then no matter how rough the flight, at least the pilots would not fall out of the plane. Arnold himself was the first to come up with the idea of goggles for fliers. He got tired of bugs flying into his eyes.

After setting up a school for army officers at College Park, Maryland, he became an instructor. He also became one of the world's first great pilots. People were astonished when Arnold set an altitude record of 6,540 feet on June 1, 1912. Only nine years after the Wright brothers' first flight, he had taken his plane more than a mile above the earth!

Four months later he flew from College Park to Washington, D. C. to Fort Myer, Virginia, then back to his home field. It was a round-trip of about thirty miles. He was also the first pilot to transport airmail letters. So what if he only had to take the mail five miles across Long Island. Within a few years other pilots would follow his lead and fly the mail across the country.

Like every other flier, Arnold had his share of close calls. He once crashed his plane into the Atlantic Ocean near Plymouth Beach, Massachusetts. He escaped drowning by hanging onto the broken craft's wing as it bobbed up and down in the water. The scar on his chin reminded him of the accident for the rest of his life.

When the United States entered World War I in 1917, Arnold was put in charge of thirty training schools for combat airmen. He did not like being stuck behind a desk; he wanted to fly. Finally, after repeated requests, he was reassigned to a combat unit. But the day he arrived in Europe, November 11, 1918, was Armistice Day, and the war was over. By then, the Army Air Service had thousands of men and hundreds of planes.

Without a war to fight, Arnold concentrated on proving to the public the value of flight. He was in charge of a military project that allowed planes to be refueled in midair. When blizzards hit parts of the Southwest, he and his fliers were the first to drop food from planes to people stranded by the snow. He even raced—and beat—a flock of pigeons from Portland, Oregon, to San Francisco, California. He also wrote books on aviation.

But then Germany, Japan, and Italy began strengthening their armed forces and seizing their neighbors' land. Many Americans feared their country would soon be dragged into the war. Arnold was put in charge of the Army Air Corps. His job was to organize and equip the Army's air force. He had barely begun when Japan bombed Pearl Harbor in 1941 and the United States was officially involved in World War II. Before the war ended less than four years later, Arnold would be commanding 2.5 million men and 75,000 planes.

But when the war began, the general had to make do with the aircraft he had. He ordered Colonel James Doolittle to come up with a surprise attack on Tokyo, Japan, using small modified B-25 bombers. On April 18, 1942, four months after Pearl Harbor, sixteen planes took off from the aircraft carrier U.S.S. *Hornet* and flew 670 miles to Tokyo where they dropped a few bombs before landing in China. The raid did little damage, but it let the Japanese know there would be a price to be paid for the attack on Pearl Harbor.

In Europe, American B-24 Liberator bombers flew long-range missions against the Germans. Unfortunately, they had to fly without an escort because fighter planes could not fly long distances. They also had to fly low to drop their bombs. The B-24s were sitting ducks for enemy fighters and antiaircraft fire. Arnold told his commanders, "This is a MUST . . . Destroy the enemy Air Force."[2]

Soon long-range fighter planes like the Thunderbolt and Mustang were put into action to protect the bombers. The Germans, on the other hand, failed to produce large numbers of their deadly Messerschmitt jets. Adolf Hitler did not think they were crucial to the war effort. "I want bombers, bombers, bombers!" he told his commanders.[3] In the climactic air war over Germany in February and March 1944, the Allies shot down eight hundred Luftwaffe planes. This destroyed the German air force.

Arnold insisted that the United States develop a super bomber that could carry more bombs and fly farther than any other aircraft. From initial planning in 1940, it took four years to design and manufacture the first B-29.

In the meantime, the most important American bomber used against Germany was the B-17 Flying Fortress. Because it carried its own machine guns, it did not need a fighter escort. It rained destruction over Europe from huge formations of fifty-four planes.

The B-29 was bigger and more effective than either the B-24 or B-25. It was a huge machine, weighing sixty tons and capable of flying sixteen hours without stopping. It also could inflict unbelievable damage.

The first B-29 Super Fortresses took off from China and India to attack Japanese installations. Flying in a close-formation developed by Major General Curtis E. LeMay, they were an extremely effective weapon. As American forces closed in on Japan, huge airfields were carved out of jungle islands in the Pacific for the B-29s. In one massive raid on August 2, 1945, 855 of the huge planes destroyed six Japanese cities.

In Europe bombing raids were initially conducted at night because it was thought that it would be safer for the pilots if they could not be seen. But Arnold decided the raids should be flown in broad daylight. He felt it was much easier for his pilots to hit targets they could see. Soon American bombs were taking a terrible toll on German industrial targets.

"There is no doubt that the Americans harmed us most," said a Luftwaffe officer after the war. "We

Arnold talks to President Franklin D. Roosevelt in Sicily, Italy, on December 8, 1943. This was less than a year before Arnold was named a five-star general.

could have stood the British attacks on our cities. But the American devastation of our airfields, factories and oil depots made it impossible for us to keep going."[4]

The war ended soon after B-29 bombers dropped atomic bombs on Hiroshima and Nagasaki, Japan. By then, the huge planes had flown 35,000 missions and dropped 175,000 tons of bombs.

In 1944, after the defeat of Germany, Arnold was named a five-star general of the Army. He would later be the first to be given the rank of five-star general of the Air Force. In 1947, a year after Arnold retired, the National Defense Act created a separate Air Force from the Army. By the time he died in Sonoma, California, on January 15, 1950, Henry Arnold's desire to see the Air Force stand as an equal with the Army and Navy had been fulfilled.

Omar N. Bradley

(1893–1981)

Omar Nelson Bradley was born in Clark, Missouri, on February 12, 1893. When he was growing up, Omar planned to attend college near his home in Missouri. But when he was fourteen, his father died, and the family had very little money. After graduation from high school, he went to work as a laborer for the Wabash Railroad so he could save enough money to pay his own tuition.

John Crewson, a Sunday school superintendent, suggested that Omar attend West Point. The young man laughed at the idea. "But I couldn't afford to go to West Point."

"You don't pay to go to West Point, Omar. The army pays you while you're there."[1]

General Omar N. Bradley

Within a few weeks, Bradley passed the entrance examination and was on his way to his new school as a member of the class of 1915. During his years at West Point, he did well in his classes and at sports. One of his teammates on the football team was Dwight D. Eisenhower. Bradley did so well at the Academy that Eisenhower said, "Some of us some day will be bragging, 'Sure, General Bradley was a classmate of mine.'"[2]

Bradley spent much of the next twenty years teaching young soldiers in South Dakota, Hawaii, and back at West Point. Early in 1941 he earned the rank of brigadier general and took command of the Infantry School at Fort Benning, Georgia.

After the United States entered World War II a few months later, the American armed services swelled as hundreds of thousands of young men enlisted or were drafted. Many of the new soldiers who arrived at Fort Benning were in no condition to fight a war. They were confused and homesick; some of them were in poor physical shape.

Bradley knew the Army needed top-notch soldiers, so he worked to lift his men's morale as soon as they arrived. He made sure the new recruits were greeted by military bands. Within minutes, they were wearing sharp new uniforms and eating a big, hot meal. He wanted his men to know that their commander cared about them, but he also wanted them to be tough. Besides their regular military training, they went through a program of rigorous physical conditioning.

Bradley hoped to accompany his soldiers to Europe where he would lead them in battle against the Germans and Italians. But he had been so successful at preparing the soldiers at Fort Benning for combat that General George C. Marshall, the Army Chief of Staff, assigned him to do the same with another division in Camp Livingston, Louisiana. It looked like Bradley might never see action himself.

Soon, however, Eisenhower decided he needed his old friend in Africa. The situation there was grim. After a huge German army led by Field Marshal Erwin Rommel had been defeated by British forces at El Alamein, Egypt, American troops were supposed to cut off their retreat by moving into Tunisia. But Rommel moved quickly and got there first in February 1943. Then it became the job of Eisenhower's inexperienced troops to push Rommel out or defeat him.

Rommel did not wait to be attacked. Instead he hit the Americans at Kasserine Pass, a thin break in the mountains. In their first major battle, Eisenhower's men faced a barrage of small German attacks. Soon thousands of Axis soldiers were pouring into the pass, and the Americans were forced to retreat.

Eisenhower was angry and embarrassed. His men had been poorly prepared, fought badly, and were whipped by Rommel. After Kasserine Pass, the question was no longer whether the Americans would push the Germans out of Tunisia. The world now watched to see if the Axis soldiers instead would push the Americans back to Algeria.

As soon as he arrived in Africa, Bradley assessed the situation. He convinced Eisenhower to replace Major General Lloyd Fredendall, the general who had been in charge of United States Forces at Kasserine Pass. Within a few weeks, Bradley himself was the new commander of II Corps, a group of tens of thousands of soldiers.

By then, there was little respect for the new fighters from the United States. The veteran German troops were confident they could beat them again. Even their British allies were worried that the Americans were not going to be much help against the Axis armies. Many were convinced that soldiers from Britain were the only ones who could stand up to the enemy.

Bradley was confident, and he was ready to fight. "The people in the United States want a victory," he told Eisenhower, "and they deserve one." He asked for the chance to lead his II Corps against Rommel. Unless his men went after the enemy, "you'll never know how good or bad we really are. And neither will the American people."[3]

The new commander had a plan: instead of waiting for the Germans to attack, the Americans would move north toward Bizerte. This would sandwich the enemy between the Mediterranean Sea to the north and the British forces moving in from the east. Their biggest obstacle would be a bare, white mound, called Hill 609. From its top, Rommel's troops could easily direct artillery fire down on Bradley's men. There was no way to get past the hill without taking it, and the German soldiers would be tough to move. High ground is an easy position to defend, and the Germans were determined to keep it. The longer they kept the Americans and British tied down in Africa, the more time the Axis forces had to prepare to defend Europe from Allied attacks.

"Get that hill," Bradley told one of his deputies, "and you'll break up the enemy's defenses clear across the front. Take it and no one will ever again doubt the toughness of your division."[4] American infantry-men charged up Hill 609, but they were repulsed by the Germans. It would take more than toughness to take the hill; it would take a smart plan.

That is when Bradley surprised the Germans by charging their position from two sides with seventeen Sherman tanks. The big tanks were not designed to move up hills, but the general knew they could do the job. As the tanks drove up the hill far enough to get the enemy positions in their sights, German machine-gun fire had no effect. Soon Hill 609 shook as the Americans' 75-millimeter guns sent shell after shell at the Germans. Within a few hours, the hill belonged to II Corps. Then thousands of American soldiers were racing toward Bizerte while the British continued to close in on Tunis. Rommel fled back home to Germany, but forty thousand of his soldiers surrendered to II Corps on May 9, 1943.

Now the Allies focused their attention on Europe. Their first attack would be made on Sicily, an Italian island in the Mediterranean Sea between Africa and Italy. Bradley helped plan and lead the attack with General George S. Patton and British general Sir Bernard Montgomery. It took just thirty-eight days to clear Sicily of Axis forces. By then Benito Mussolini had been overthrown. Soon the Americans and British advanced on Italy itself. On September 3, 1943, Italy surrendered. Germany stood alone in Europe against the combined forces of the United States, Great Britain, and the Soviet Union.

Eisenhower decided the invasion of occupied France would be made on the English Channel coastline of Normandy, France. Bradley was given command of the United States First Army. His men would attempt to take the western half of the long beachhead. Their two main landing points were nicknamed Omaha Beach and Utah Beach. At the same time British and Canadian troops would be landing farther west on the Normandy coast at Sword Beach, Juno Beach, and Gold Beach.

It was Bradley's idea to drop airborne troops further inland behind the enemy line. He hoped the paratroopers would distract the Germans and delay them from sending reinforcements to the beaches, where the main thrust of the British and the

American attack would be occurring. Bradley had a solid plan and prepared his men well.

When the Americans landed at Utah Beach, they met little resistance, so they immediately charged inland. Before nightfall, they had advanced six miles.

It was a different story at Omaha Beach. Rough seas sank ten landing craft and twenty-one of the twenty-nine tanks before they could even reach the shore. The steep bluffs facing the beach were fortified by heavy German artillery, and there were many more enemy soldiers than had been expected. Many of the Americans were mowed down by machine-gun fire as soon as their boat ramps opened. It looked like a disaster.

Bradley had to decide what to do. Should he pull his troops out of a hopeless situation at Omaha? They could instead be sent to follow the initial landings at Utah or to assist the British farther east on the Normandy coast. But, despite the problems, the general retained confidence in his plans—and in his soldiers.

Colonel George A. Taylor and his men made it to the beach, but they were under incredible fire. "Two kinds of people are staying on this beach," he yelled, "the dead and those who are going to die. Now let's get . . . out of here."[5] Within two hours of the landing, the first Americans reached the bluff. Soon they broke through.

The Allies began pushing into France, but after the initial success of D-day, the Germans regrouped and the Americans, British, and Canadians seemed to be bottled up in Normandy. Bradley said the Allied strategy had to be simple: "We want to smash right on through."[6] To accomplish that, he came up with Operation Cobra. The German stronghold at St. Lo, a French village, was hit with a devastating air attack. When it was over, the German commander said, "Nothing was visible but dust and smoke." The way was clear for the Allies to break through the German lines across northern France. By the end of August, Paris, the French capital, had been liberated from the Germans.

The Allies moved steadily across Europe until the Battle of the Bulge in December when German troops beat back the Americans in Belgium and Luxembourg with a surprise attack. But Adolf Hitler's troops did not have the men or the supplies to sustain a long offensive. Within two weeks, the Germans were on the run.

After the Battle of the Bulge, it was just a matter of time as the British, Russians, and Americans closed in on Hitler. To slow down their advances, the Germans planned to destroy the bridges that crossed the important Rhine River. Bradley was delighted when the Ludendorff Bridge at Remagen was discovered intact in March 1945. "Hot dog," he said. "This will bust him wide open! . . . Shove everything you can across it."[7] Troops and supplies poured across the bridge. A month later the war in Europe was over.

Bradley stands in full uniform, ready to speak.

Bradley later became administrator of Veterans Affairs in Washington, D.C., from 1945 to 1947. He was in charge of programs that helped millions of veterans. He then became Army Chief of Staff (1948–1949) and went on the be the first chairman of the Joint Chiefs of Staff (1949–1953). In 1951 he published *A Soldier's Story.*

After his retirement in 1953, Bradley lived out the rest of his life in the private sector. He died on April 8, 1981, in New York City.

By that time his past inspirational leadership and his concern for the common soldiers had made him one of the most popular generals in American history. As his friend George S. Patton said after D-day, "Brad had really pulled a great show, and should get credit for it."[8]

General Dwight D. Eisenhower

Dwight D. Eisenhower
(1890–1969)

Dwight David Eisenhower was born into a poor family on October 14, 1890, in Denison, Texas. While living in Abilene, Kansas, the Eisenhowers were so poor that Dwight, or "Little Ike," once had to wear his mother's high-button shoes to school when his wore out. To make ends meet, the Eisenhower boys sold vegetables they grew in their big yard.

When he was a freshman in high school, Ike slipped while racing his friends. He scraped his left knee on a board, but the injury did not seem serious until that night. A fever developed, and he had trouble staying awake. The doctor said he was suffering from blood poisoning. If his condition did not improve, the leg would have to be amputated—or he might die.

"I became alarmed, and even furious," Eisenhower remembered. He made his brother, Edgar, promise not to let the doctor cut off the leg. "I'd rather be dead than crippled, and not be able to play ball."[1] Edgar stood guard at the bedroom door, and allowed the doctor to enter only to change medicines. After a few days, Ike began to improve without an amputation, but he was too sick to return to school until the next fall when he had to repeat ninth grade.

After high school, a friend persuaded Eisenhower to take the entrance examinations for the Military and Naval Academies. He passed both and decided to attend West Point.

In his second year as a cadet, Eisenhower was well on his way to becoming a star on the Army football team. *The New York Times* said he could be "one of the best backs in the East."[2] But in a game against Carlisle, with the great Jim Thorpe, Eisenhower twisted his knee. More football and rigorous military drills aggravated the injury, and soon it was painfully swollen. He had to spend a month in the hospital while the knee mended. He was forced to give up football, but he became a cheerleader and an assistant coach for the team.

Because of the knee injury, the Army almost did not give Eisenhower a commission when he graduated from West Point. It was feared that he might not be able to move around well enough to be an active officer. When his future was in doubt, he made plans to travel to Argentina. If he did not get his commission, he thought he might like to live in South America. Luckily, the Army decided to take a risk on Eisenhower. He became a second lieutenant in 1915.

During World War I, the young officer worked at army bases in Georgia, Kansas, Maryland, and Pennsylvania where he trained troops and organized crews to fight in Europe. Eisenhower, of course, did not want to train or organize; he wanted to lead men into battle. But, he said, "every one of my frantic efforts to get to the scene of action had been defeated."[3] At last he received orders to leave the United States for France, but a week before his departure, the war suddenly ended.

Eisenhower then served in the Panama Canal Zone before attending the Command and General Staff School in Fort Leavenworth, Kansas. Out of 275 officers, he graduated at the top of his class.

In 1933 he was sent to the Philippines as an assistant to General Douglas MacArthur, the island nation's military advisor. Six years later, Eisenhower asked to be reassigned to the United States after Germany invaded Poland. "I believe we're going to get into this war," he said, "and I'm going home to try to help do my part in preparing for it."[4]

Before leaving the Philippines, he put together a detailed plan for defending the islands in the event of a Japanese invasion. "There is one line," he wrote, "and one only, at which the defending forces will enjoy a tremendous advantage over any attack on land. That line is the beach. Successful penetration of a defended beach is the most difficult operation in warfare."[5] That, of course, is exactly the type of operation he would command five years later on D-day when thousands of Allied soldiers would attempt to take the beaches of Normandy from the Germans.

To prepare American troops for possible entry into the war, four hundred thousand soldiers took part in war maneuvers in Louisiana in September 1941. The maneuvers were not real combat, just "war games." They gave the soldiers and their generals practice at moving men and developing strategy. Eisenhower was the Chief of Staff for the side that won the games. He was the man who devised the plan that thwarted the enemy. He impressed many people with his skill at organization and outwitting his opponents.

After the Japanese attacked Pearl Harbor three months later and the United States entered the real war, General George C. Marshall, the Army Chief of Staff, called Eisenhower to Washington, D.C. He asked him to prepare a Pacific war plan against the Japanese. After a few hours, Eisenhower told him that the Allies could probably not stop Japan from taking the Philippines. The most important thing to do right away was to build up Australia as the main base from which to fight the enemy. Supplies could be funneled into the island through Hawaii, Fiji,

New Zealand, and New Caledonia. Eventually, the Allies would be strong enough in the Pacific to begin recapturing land from the Japanese.

"I agree with you," Marshall said. "Do your best to save them."[6] So Eisenhower drew up detailed plans for the war against Japan. Soon he was in charge of the war department's plans division. Next Marshall sent him to England, where he developed a plan for a united command of Allied troops in Europe. When the Chief of Staff saw how well Eisenhower was able to gain the trust and cooperation of the British, Marshall made him the commanding general of the European Theater of Operations.

His first major campaign was against Field Marshal Erwin Rommel and thousands of entrenched German soldiers in North Africa. With men like George S. Patton and Omar N. Bradley under him as his field commanders, Eisenhower successfully pushed Rommel out of Africa. After the victory, he was not ready to celebrate. "Ike is nonchalant," wrote one of his assistants. "For him this battle was finished some time ago; now his thoughts are on the next job against Hitler—Sicily."[7]

He decided the first step to the island of Sicily off the coast of Italy would be heavy naval artillery fire on Axis air bases on the islands of Pantelleria and Lampedusa. Some of his officers thought the plan was a mistake; they did not feel the islands could be taken without a direct invasion. But Eisenhower's plan worked, and soon the Allies were using the islands as air bases for the Allies.

Patton and Sir Bernard Montgomery, the British general, worked together to take Sicily in just thirty-eight days. That defeat helped drive Italy's dictator, Benito Mussolini, from power. An armistice was signed, and Italy was out of the war. The German army, however, continued to occupy the country.

Then Eisenhower began to concentrate on the planning of Operation Overlord, the invasion of France. But who would be in charge? Marshall himself had hopes of coming to England to direct the huge operation, but President Franklin D. Roosevelt had other ideas. Late in 1943, when the president met Eisenhower in Cairo, Egypt, he told him, "Well, Ike, you are going to command Overlord."[8]

The D-day landings were set for June 5, 1944, but a terrible storm on the English Channel postponed the invasion. The biggest army in history—one million men, four thousand ships and eleven thousand planes—was ready to go. Eisenhower did not want them to wait any longer. After looking over weather reports and checking out the sky himself, he said, "Well, we'll go."[9]

Those three words unleashed a barrage of Allied power against the German-held beaches of Normandy on June 6, 1944. Many times the general must have remembered what he had written in the Philippines about the difficulties of attacking a fortified beach.

The success of Operation Overlord was never a foregone conclusion. The Germans were surprised by the timing and location of the invasion, but they had been preparing for it for years. They had thousands of troops and huge fortifications in place. Some of the early landings, particularly at Omaha Beach, were extremely difficult. In case of failure, the commander was ready to accept full responsibility. Eisenhower had prepared a brief announcement:

> Our landings . . . have failed and I have withdrawn the troops. My decision to attack . . . was based upon the best information available. The troops, the air and the Navy, did all that bravery and devotion to duty could do. If any blame or fault attaches to the attempt, it is mine alone.[10]

But after a few hours, it was clear the landings were successful. The beaches were secured by soldiers led by Montgomery, Bradley, and Patton. By the end of June, Bradley's troops broke out of Normandy as part of Operation Cobra. Soon Allied troops were racing across France for Germany.

Winston Churchill, England's leader, wished Eisenhower luck, but said he would be lucky just to have his divisions safely in France by the winter of 1944–45. "If in addition to this you have . . . freed beautiful Paris from the enemy, I will assert the victory to be the greatest of modern times."[11] Eisenhower's troops liberated Paris and most of France by the end of the summer.

In December 1944 he was promoted to 5 star rank as general of the Army.

Eleven months after D-day, Alfred Jodl, Germany's military leader after Hitler's suicide, stood before Eisenhower. "Do you understand the terms of the document of surrender you have just signed?" the commander asked.

"Yes."

"You will get instructions at a later date. And you will be expected to carry them out faithfully."

The German nodded.

"That is all."[12]

After the defeated general left the room, Eisenhower finally smiled. The war was over. Quickly he dispatched a simple message to Washington: "The mission of this allied force was fulfilled at 0241, local time, May 7, 1945. Eisenhower."[13]

After the war, in 1945, Eisenhower replaced Marshall as Army Chief of Staff. During this time he suggested that there be a single commander for all armed forces. In 1947 Congress compromised with him by putting a single secretary of defense in charge of all armed forces.

After retiring from the Army, he became president of Columbia University in New York. In 1948, he published a successful book, *Crusade in Europe*, about his war experiences. Then in 1950 he returned to active service to become Supreme Commander of the North Atlantic Treaty Organization (NATO) forces in Europe.

Eisenhower (front middle) with General Omar N. Bradley (second from left) and General S. Patton (left) in Belgium in 1944. Bradley and Patton helped execute Eisenhower's D-day invasion.

In 1952 Eisenhower was elected to the first of his two terms as president of the United States. While president he dealt with such problems as the threat of communism, the Suez Canal Crises, and the U-2 incident with the same kind of careful decision making that had made him a great general.

After his second term, Eisenhower retired and wrote three more books about his life. He died of heart failure on March 28, 1969, in Washington, D.C. Today he remains one of the most popular figures in American history.

Curtis E. LeMay

(1906–1990)

Curtis Emerson LeMay was born on November 15, 1906, in Columbus, Ohio. Curtis saw his first airplane before he was six years old. It was an early "flying machine," probably a biwinged craft with an open cockpit. "It came from nowhere," LeMay remembered,

> There it was and I wanted to catch it . . . . I just thought that I might be able to grab the airplane and have it for my own. . . . So I lit out after it . . . Ran as fast as I could, across neighbors' lawns, across gardens and vacant lots, sometimes on the sidewalk, sometimes in the street.[1]

Little Curtis never caught the plane, but he never forgot it either.

General Curtis E. LeMay

As a teenager he was a quiet young man who was not afraid to work. To earn money he sold newspapers and later worked in an iron foundry. But he kept dreaming of flying. When LeMay failed to get an appointment to West Point, he enrolled at Ohio State University, where he joined the Reserve Officers' Training Corps (ROTC).

After graduation, he joined the United States Army and became an excellent pilot. In May 1938 as part of a military exercise, he led three B-17s over the ocean for seven hundred miles to find a cruise ship. For a pilot utilizing only a compass, it was a very impressive feat.

Four years later, he was a bomber commander in Europe. The Allies had decided that the best way to use air power was to pound German factories. If their weapons and machines could not be produced, the Axis powers would be in trouble.

To do the job, the Americans decided to use the B-17 Flying Fortress. It was a big, relatively new plane with a wingspan of 103 feet. The B-17 could carry a heavy load of bombs higher and faster than any other bomber. It could also deliver the bombs with almost-pinpoint accuracy.

But LeMay, who knew the B-17 well, realized it was extremely vulnerable to enemy attacks. When a group was flying in formation, the Germans could drop a bomb from above that could take out several aircraft. But their most effective tactic was to attack the B-17 head on. German Luftwaffe pilots would charge straight at the nose of the planes and unleash a short burst of machine-gun fire just before rolling away from the formation and barely avoiding a collision. The attack usually killed the B-17 pilot and caused enough damage to down the big plane.

"After we had been under constant attack for a solid hour," said an American pilot, "it appeared certain that [our] group was faced with annihilation. Seven of our group had been shot down, the sky was still mottled with rising fighters. . . . I had long since mentally accepted the fact of death."[2] That pilot was lucky; he made it back.

Even though he was a commander, during his early days in Europe, LeMay joined his men in the dangerous attacks. "We came into this war fresh," he said. "How can any commanding officer send his people into combat when he knows nothing about it? So I started leading all missions personally. . . . You have to get in there and fight to find out what it's all about."[3]

LeMay's superiors eventually ordered him to stay on the ground, but he worried constantly about the safety of his men and the success of their missions. In his office he used small B-17 models to figure out new strategies to reduce casualties. The formation he devised involved three groups of eighteen aircraft stacked on top of each other. By flying tightly together, the planes could more easily protect each other. Each B-17 also got a new gun installed just below its nose.

When the formation arrived at the target, the lead plane dropped a smoke marker with its bombs. The other fifty-three planes aimed their bombs at the billowing smoke. This strategy allowed the B-17 formations to accurately concentrate their attacks while increasing their chances of returning safely. The success of the B-17 attacks was a big factor in the destruction of the German war effort.

When the war in Europe ended in 1945, LeMay went to the Pacific to help coordinate air attacks on Japan. American forces there were using a brand new plane, the B-29 Super Fortress. It was bigger and faster than the B-17. With extra fuel tanks, it had a range of 4,100 miles and a top speed of 364 miles per hour.

Unfortunately, the engines of the early models tended to catch fire, and the planes flew so high that it was hard for the pilots to spot their targets if there were clouds. They were usually attacked by suicide fighter planes that purposely rammed into them. Many B-29s and their eleven-man crews were lost late in 1944.

When LeMay arrived in the Pacific, he experimented with different formations, but the heavy losses continued. Then on December 18, he tried a new strategy when he sent eighty-four B-29s against a Japanese dockyard in Hankow, China. He had them fly lower, and he loaded most of them with incendiary bombs. The American pilots were able to hit their targets more accurately, and it was tougher

LeMay helped coordinate air attacks on Japan after the war in Europe ended.

for the Japanese defenders to hit them. The dockyard was destroyed and most of the American planes returned safely.

Six weeks later, LeMay's planes attacked Japan itself, burning down five factories in Kobe. The success of that attack convinced him that incendiary bombs would be much more deadly than conventional high-explosive ammunition. Much of Japan's industry was spread out in small workshops scattered throughout major cities. The cities themselves were crowded places, filled with wooden buildings. They were perfect targets for fire bombs.

Hitting Japan's cities would result in thousands of civilian deaths, but LeMay said that that could not be avoided. "The entire population got into the act and worked to make those airplanes or munitions of war . . . men, women, children. We knew we were going to kill a lot of women and kids. . . . Had to be done."[4]

LeMay lost patience with those who argued against his strategy: "No matter how you slice it, you're going to kill an awful lot of civilians. Thousands and thousands." The only alternative was to invade Japan, an attack that might claim a million American lives. "We're at war with Japan. We were attacked by Japan. Do you want to kill Japanese, or would you rather have Americans killed?"[5]

To reduce civilian casualties, LeMay's forces dropped thousands of leaflets that warned, "Your city has been listed for destruction by our powerful air forces. . . . Systematic destruction of city after city will continue as long as you blindly follow your military leaders whose blunders have placed you on the very brink of oblivion. . . . We urge all civilians to evacuate at once."[6] At first the Japanese paid little attention to the warnings, but after the initial attacks, they realized that LeMay meant business. "The rest [of the warned cities] were practically depopulated in nothing flat," LeMay wrote.[7]

The firebombing was a simple but deadly process. The first B-29 dropped a napalm canister that exploded about one hundred feet above the ground. This started dozens of small fires. The other planes followed, dropping hundreds of small canisters, which exploded in the air, drenching the area with oil, which fueled the flames. Wave after wave of bombers dropped more and more oil; the flames grew higher and hotter.

Tokyo, Japan's capital, was firebombed on the nights of March 9–10, 1945. "As I ran, I kept my eyes on the sky," said Fusako Sasaki. "It was like a fireworks display as the incendiaries exploded . . . People were aflame, rolling and writhing in agony, screaming piteously for help."[8]

Sasaki was one of the lucky ones who survived. Winds blew the huge walls of fire at speeds up to 40 miles per hour. The flames could be seen from 150 miles away. The fires burned for four days, gutting sixteen square miles of the city. As many as two hundred thousand people were burned to death. Almost 2 million were left homeless.

LeMay's men suffered few casualties during the Tokyo attack. Of the 325 planes, only 14 were lost.

The attacks continued for the next five months. Every other night as many as five hundred B-29s took off from American bases. At least half a million Japanese were killed in attacks on twenty-six cities, and 13 million lost their homes.

LeMay was convinced the incendiary bombing could destroy Japan's ability to continue the war. Without factories that made military supplies, their soldiers would be unable to fight. The civilian deaths, he believed, would convince the Japanese to give up. Then there would be no need for horrible American losses in an invasion.

But the general never got to see if his strategy would work. Atomic bombs, not incendiaries, convinced the Japanese leadership that the war must end.

After World War II, LeMay became part of the United States Air Force when it separated from the Army. He commanded the Strategic Air Command from 1948 to 1957 which carried, but never dropped, atomic bombs. He also served as Air Force Chief of Staff and finally retired as a four-star general in 1965.

LeMay became a focus of controversy during the Vietnam War when he suggested that the war could be won if the United States was willing to use tactical atomic bombs. In 1968 presidential hopeful George Wallace chose him as the vice-presidential candidate of the American Independent Party.

LeMay talked tough, and his tactics were tough, too, but they were usually very effective. Early in World War II, one of his commanding generals recognized that he was not always a popular officer, but that he got things done: "He may not be human, but when I can find a hundred other group commanders like him, we'll get on with this air war. We might even win it."[9]

On October 1, 1990, Curtis E. LeMay died at March Air Force Base, California.

Douglas MacArthur

(1880–1964)

During World War I, when he was a lieutenant in France, Douglas MacArthur was known as "the dude." Nobody else dressed the way he did. Instead of a steel helmet and a regulation uniform, he wore a crushed cap, a black turtleneck sweater, riding breeches, a four-foot scarf knitted by his mother, and shiny boots. Instead of a weapon, he carried a riding crop to slap his horse. Usually he had a cigarette in a long holder sticking out of his mouth.

Why did MacArthur go out of his way to break regulations and display his personal sense of style? "It's the orders you disobey that make you famous," he explained.[1]

Born on January 26, 1880, in Little Rock, Arkansas, MacArthur dressed dramatically all his life.

General Douglas MacArthur

He also had a flair for theatrically describing his opinions and his experiences. "We moved out in the misty dawn, and from then on little units of our men crawled and sneaked and side-slipped forward from one bit of cover to another," was how he described the beginnings of a battle. "Death, cold and remorseless, whistled its way through our ranks."[2]

But MacArthur was much more than an eccentric dresser and an exciting writer; he was a fearless soldier. During World War I, he received nine citations for bravery and was wounded several times.

The MacArthurs knew battle well. Douglas's father, Arthur, was awarded America's highest decoration, the Congressional Medal of Honor, for bravery when he served in the Union Army during the Civil War. Douglas was raised in frontier posts where his father was an officer in the fight against Indians.

After graduation from West Point, Douglas followed his father and became an Army officer. During World War I, he was very popular with the men who served under him. When in battle, he encouraged them to call him Buddy. MacArthur never forgot the brave soldiers he fought with in France. "I can see them now," he said years later. "Forming grimly for the attack, blue-lipped, covered with sludge and mud, chilled by the wind and rain of the foxhole . . . I do not know the dignity of their birth, but I do know the glory of their death."[3]

In 1918 when he was only thirty-eight, he attained the rank of brigadier general. When the war ended, he became superintendent of West Point. In 1920 he was named America's youngest division commander. He later served five years as Army Chief of Staff, the same post his father had held decades before.

In 1935 the general was appointed military advisor to the Philippines, a nation of more than seven thousand islands in the Pacific Ocean near the Asian mainland. The Philippines was a commonwealth of the United States, with its own government. President Manuel Quezon appointed MacArthur field marshal and commander of his country's tiny army. The general retired from the American Army to devote full time to his work in the Philippines. To beef up the commonwealth's army, MacArthur proposed universal military service for its young men.

In July of 1941 the general was recalled to active duty with the United States Army. He was still in the Philippines five months later when the Japanese bombed Pearl Harbor. The same day, Clark Field, an American base in the Philippines was also attacked. After the war, Japanese officers said they had to attack before MacArthur finished building up the Philippine armed forces: "The Japanese had to intervene before it was too late."[4]

But the general was surprised by the suddenness of the attack. Even though he knew of the assault on Pearl Harbor, MacArthur's planes were sitting in neat rows at Clark Field when the Japanese arrived. A third of them were destroyed.[5]

Soon thousands of Japanese troops invaded the island. American and Philippine soldiers were outnumbered and undersupplied. "My heart ached as I saw my men slowly wasting away," MacArthur wrote about the battle. "Their clothes hung on them like tattered rags. Their bare feet stuck out in silent protest."[6]

But some of his troops who were in good shape with plenty of supplies, still fought poorly. Thousands of fresh Philippine soldiers abandoned their weapons and disappeared into the countryside near the beach as the enemy invaded.

MacArthur, his wife and young son, and his staff withdrew to Corregidor, an island just off the capital of Manila. As the Japanese closed in, General George C. Marshall suggested that the general evacuate his wife and son, but MacArthur said, "I and my family will share the fate of the garrison."[7]

He carried a small derringer with him and said, "They will never take me alive." He did not believe he would survive. "I fully expected to be killed," he said later. "I would never have surrendered."[8]

President Franklin D. Roosevelt did not want to lose one of his most famous generals. While he admired MacArthur's courage and determination to fight on with his men, he believed the general's leadership would be needed later in the war when more men and supplies would be available to fight the Japanese. MacArthur left the Philippines on March 11.

"The President . . . ordered me to break through the Japanese lines and proceed from Corregidor to Australia. . . . I came through and I shall return."[9] Those last three words were not forgotten by the Filipinos who saw the Japanese conquer their country soon after MacArthur's departure. They would wait and hope for MacArthur's return with an American force.

His words also inspired the Australians who watched the enemy get closer and closer to their own land: "We shall win or we shall die, and to this end I pledge you the full resources of all the mighty power of my country and all the blood of my country-men."[10]

In 1942 MacArthur was named supreme Allied commander in the East Indies, Australia, and the Philippines. He disagreed with the strategy of concentrating Allied strength in Europe until Adolf Hitler was defeated. He asked for forces for the Pacific. Working with the limited resources available to him, MacArthur helped devise a strategy to defeat the Japanese by "island hopping."

Instead of attempting to recapture each island, the Allies would try to take just the biggest, most important ones. The skipped islands, still in Japanese hands, would be left to "wither on the vine." Without nearby reinforcements, they would eventually be forced to surrender, too.

Over the next few months, many of these islands—Midway, Guadalcanal, Attu, Salamaua, and Lae—became familiar to people around the world as fierce battles were waged for them. The Allies, taking back the islands one by one, were turning the tables on the Japanese. Finally they were fighting again for control of the Philippines.

In October 1944 MacArthur kept his promise by wading ashore at Leyte, one of the Philippine islands. "People of the Philippines," he said, "I have returned . . . We have come, dedicated and committed to the task of destroying every vestige of enemy control over your daily lives, and of restoring upon a foundation of indestructible strength, the liberties of your people."[11]

For his efforts in the defense of the Philippines, the general was awarded the Congressional Medal of Honor. Arthur and Douglas MacArthur are the only father and son to both receive their nation's highest military honor.

Slowly, steadily, Allied forces closed in on Japan itself. MacArthur expected to lead hundreds of thousands of men in a massive invasion. But in August 1945 the atomic bombs dropped on Hiroshima and Nagasaki brought an abrupt end to the war. There would be no need for an Allied invasion of Japan.

On September 2, 1945, MacArthur accepted the Japanese surrender on the American battleship U.S.S. *Missouri* in Tokyo Bay. "Today the guns are silent," he said. "A great tragedy has ended. A great victory has been won. The skies no longer rain death."[12]

President Harry S Truman named the general Supreme Allied Commander in Japan. By his efforts to rebuild their defeated nation, MacArthur earned the respect and admiration of many Japanese. He dismantled their armed forces while supervising the writing of a new, democratic constitution.

But when the Korean War erupted in the summer of 1950, President Truman named him the commanding general of the United Nations forces battling against North Korea, which had invaded South Korea. MacArthur turned the tide with a daring landing at Inchon, South Korea, behind enemy lines and almost won the war. But the North Koreans were saved when China, now a Communist country, entered the war and sent reinforcements and planes to their aid.

MacArthur suggested the use of bombs, perhaps even atomic ones, against China. Truman and many civilian officials felt that direct attacks on China could result in World War III. The two men did not get along; the president did not even like the way the general had dressed when they met at Wake Island. "He was wearing . . . sunglasses and a shirt that was unbuttoned . . . I never did understand . . . an old man like that and a five-star general to boot, why he went around dressed up like a nineteen-year-old second lieutenant."[13]

MacArthur with President Harry S Truman. After the war, Truman appointed MacArthur Supreme Allied Commander of Japan.

The general publicly complained about Truman's policies, which he claimed were keeping him from winning the war. In April 1951 the president had had enough. "General MacArthur," he said, "had openly defied the policy of the Commander in Chief, the President of the United States."[14] The general was fired.

Back in the United States, MacArthur was a hero. He received ticker tape parades and addressed both Houses of Congress. He closed his speech by quoting an old army song, "'Old soldiers never die, they just fade away.'

"And like the old soldier of that ballad, I now close my military career and just fade away—an old soldier who tried to do his duty as God gave him the light to see that duty."[15]

After the parades were over, MacArthur faded away from public attention. He lived quietly in New York City the last thirteen years of his life until his death on April 5, 1964.

George C. Marshall

(1880–1959)

Once President Franklin D. Roosevelt made the mistake of calling his top general "George."

"It's 'General Marshall,' Mr. President" was the instant reply.[1] General George Catlett Marshall commanded respect—even from the president of the United States.

But things were different when he was a teenager. Born on December 31, 1880, in Uniontown, Pennsylvania, George was a shy, awkward boy who did not work hard in school. When he was sixteen and wanted to enroll in the tough Virginia Military Institute (VMI), his older brother, Stuart, was disgusted. "That boy," he told his mother, "will disgrace this entire family if he's allowed to go."[2]

General George C. Marshall

But George went to VMI and did quite well. After graduation, he began to distinguish himself in the Army. When he was a colonel during World War I, he prepared the complicated strategy that allowed American forces to win an important battle at St.-Mihiel. General John J. Pershing, the American commander, was impressed: "It seldom happens in war that plans can be so precisely carried out as was possible in this instance."[3]

Two decades later, just before the start of World War II, Roosevelt appointed Marshall Army Chief of Staff. Even with battles raging in Europe, Africa, and Asia, most Americans hoped that their country could stay out of the war. Marshall shared their hope, but he believed the nation must be prepared to fight just in case. The world had changed since World War I. Adolf Hitler had already shown that he would attack suddenly, without warning. Modern weapons like tanks and bombers made it easy for war to spread quickly. What if the United States was the victim of a surprise attack and was forced to enter the war?

Marshall and Roosevelt tried to convince the Congress—and the country—that steps had to be taken to prepare America for war. "I do emphatically believe that the safety of this country is imperiled," the general said.[4]

Soon the United States had its first peacetime draft; thousands of young men were inducted into the armed services. From a low of 174,000, the Army grew to 1.5 million men. Billions of dollars were spent on weapons, ammunition, and supplies. When the Japanese bombed Pearl Harbor on December 7, 1941, the United States was far more ready for war than it had been two years earlier.

For the next four years, Marshall helped direct the strategy and preparation for war. He felt that American troops needed to be able to move quickly and decisively with the most modern weapons. He pushed for development of vehicles like the jeep and the two-and-a-half-ton truck, both of which would prove to be crucial.

The enormous resources of the United States would also have to be used to help Great Britain. While Marshall was pushing for increased production of weapons for American troops, the British troops in Africa were in trouble. "Send us as many Sherman tanks as you can spare," Winston Churchill begged.

"It is a terrible thing to take the weapons out of [an American] soldier's hands," the general answered. "Nevertheless, if the British need is so great, then they must have them. And we could let them have a hundred 105-millimeter self-propelled guns besides."[5]

Marshall had a simple battle plan for beating the Axis Powers: first, destroy Germany in Europe, then beat Japan in the Pacific. Roosevelt approved the plan, although they both knew it would be years before the Allies could put together the manpower to mount a full-fledged invasion of Europe.

It was not going to be easy to transport American men and equipment across the Atlantic Ocean. In the first six months of 1942, German U-boats sank 568 Allied ships. The general was worried: "The losses by submarines off our Atlantic seaboard and in the Caribbean now threaten our entire war effort."[6] He suggested the use of convoys to protect large groups of ships making their way to Europe. Gradually Allied losses dropped.

At the same time, the British suggested that the Americans send troops to help them against the Germans in Africa. Marshall was opposed. He felt action in Africa was a waste of American lives and supplies which should be saved for the major effort in Europe. However, he was overruled by Roosevelt, who believed the British desperately needed assistance. Operation Torch brought American troops to Africa.

General Douglas MacArthur argued that the Allies should not delay major action in the Pacific until after Germany was defeated. However, on this question, Roosevelt sided with Marshall.

When resources became available for major action in the Pacific, some felt that the way to Japan was an attack through China. Marshall and China's Chiang Kai-shek convinced Roosevelt that victory could be achieved more quickly by attacking Japan directly.

When it came time to plan the invasion of Europe, Marshall hoped to take personal command

President Roosevelt talks to Marshall (left). As Army Chief of Staff, Marshall worked closely with the president. General Henry H. Arnold sits to the right of Roosevelt.

of the force. But Roosevelt instead chose General Dwight D. Eisenhower, the man who had led Operation Torch in Africa. "I feel I could not sleep at night with you out of the country," the president told Marshall.[7] The Chief of Staff was too valuable to the entire war effort to let him concentrate on just one aspect of the action. The general was disappointed, but said nothing.

The D-day landings were successful, leading to the defeat of Germany in May 1945. Marshall congratulated Eisenhower: "You have made history, great history for the good of mankind and you have stood for all we hope for and admire in an officer of the United States Army."[8]

In December 1944, along with Eisenhower and MacArthur, Marshall was made a general of the Army, five-star rank.

When the fighting in Europe ceased, Marshall told the troops, "You have composed the greatest military team in history. . . . A bitter struggle is now in progress in the Pacific. We must do all in our power to terminate the fighting, to end the sacrifice of lives and starvation and oppression of peoples all over the world."[9]

After the war ended three months later, the new president, Harry S Truman, sent Marshall to China to try to mediate the ongoing dispute between Chiang's Nationalists and Mao Zedong's Communists. Despite his efforts, civil war continued, finally ending with a Communist victory in 1948.

In 1947 Marshall became the first military officer to serve as secretary of state. After six years of war, much of Europe, victors and losers alike, was in shambles. The situation was so bad that millions of people were in danger of starving. Marshall proposed a multi-billion dollar program, which would send funds to help the ravaged countries rebuild. The program's official name was the Economic Cooperation Administration (ECA), but it was much better known as the Marshall Plan.

Churchill called it "the most unsordid act in history."[10] The generous plan was a success. After presiding over the mightiest military operation in the history of the world, Marshall was in charge of a program that helped repair much of the damage World War II had caused. For his efforts, he was awarded the 1953 Nobel Peace Prize. The general closed out his long career of public service with a year as secretary of defense during the Korean War in 1950–51. Marshall died on October 16, 1959, in Washington D.C.

His death reminded the world of his accomplishments. General Omar N. Bradley pointed out that Marshall held the World War II effort together by uniting powerful leaders in Congress and the armed services as well as the leaders of the Allied countries. "In the midst of unprecedented pressures and shattering difficulties, General George C. Marshall developed the largest and most successful fighting force this country has ever seen."[11]

Truman was more direct: "A lot of them had big parades after the war, a lot of the generals, but there was never a parade for General Marshall, and he deserved it more than all the rest put together. I gave him a decoration or two, but there wasn't a decoration anywhere that would have been big enough for General Marshall."[12]

According to the president, the general's contribution could be summed up simply: "He won the war."[13]

General George S. Patton stands with General Dwight D. Eisenhower (left).

George S. Patton

(1885–1945)

George Smith Patton, Jr. was born on November 11, 1885, in San Gabriel, California. One of the first things young George had to fight was his own dyslexia, a learning disability. When he tried to read, words and letters seemed to be upside down or reversed. He worked hard at his schoolwork, but it still took him five years, not four, to graduate from West Point. Eventually, he overcame his dyslexia to become a reasonably good reader and a fine writer.

Patton always believed in being tough. If you worked harder than anybody else, he thought, you could accomplish your goals. When he was a commander, he expected a lot out of his men. "You must work unceasingly, regardless of sleep, regardless of food," he told them. "A pint of sweat will save a gallon of blood."[1]

In 1912 he competed in the modern pentathlon at the Olympic Games in Stockholm, Sweden. There were five events, one right after the other, to test the athletes' horse-riding, running, swimming, marksmanship, and fencing skills. Patton won the fencing event and finished third in riding, but he had to be helped out of the pool after a 300-meter swim. He finished the 4,000-meter run, but collapsed at the finish. At pistol shooting, which should have been his strongest event, he finished a disappointing twenty-first. His totals in the five events put him fifth overall. He was embarrassed by his shooting performance and continued to practice for the rest of his life.

Patton enjoyed athletic competition, but there was something else that was even better. As he put it later, "Battle is the most magnificent competition in which a human being can indulge!"[2]

In 1916 Pancho Villa, a Mexican revolutionary, crossed the border into Columbus, New Mexico, where he killed American soldiers and civilians. President Woodrow Wilson ordered General John J. Pershing to attack Villa's troops. Patton, then a cavalry officer, did not want to be left out. For forty hours, waiting for a chance to talk to the general, he sat in Pershing's office. When the two men finally met, Patton said, "If you take me, sir, I can promise you'll never regret it."[3] Pershing was impressed; he took Patton to Mexico.

The young officer was on patrol with six soldiers in two automobiles when they were attacked by three of Villa's men on horseback. Patton pulled his pistols, shot two of the attackers and killed them both. Then he tied the bodies to the hood of his car and drove back to see Pershing. The general immediately promoted Patton to first lieutenant.

When World War I broke out in Europe, he was ordered to set up America's first tank corps. The tank was a new weapon, and the first ones were not very effective; they were slow and clumsy with very thin armor-plating, but Patton was sure they would be an important weapon in the years to come. He called them "a means of inflicting the maximum casualties on the enemy while keeping American casualties at a minimum."[4]

In a battle in France against the Germans, Patton's tanks were stopped by long trenches dug into the ground. Men were sent with shovels to clear the way, but when machine-gun fire rang out, they dove into the trenches. Patton was furious. He raced to the tanks himself, grabbed a shovel, and started digging. Most of his troops jumped up and followed his example. When one man tried to stay in a trench, Patton hit him in the helmet with his shovel.

Soon the way was cleared and the tanks moved forward. "Let's go get them," Patton told his men. "Who is with me?"[5] With the machine guns still firing, he and six soldiers followed the tanks on foot. He did not stop until he was shot in the thigh. As he lay bleeding on the ground, he continued to call out directions to his men and pointed out the location of the enemy gunners. When he was finally taken to a hospital, he was disappointed that the Germans seemed about to surrender. "Peace is possible," he wrote his wife, Bea, "but I rather hope not for I would like to have a few more fights."[6]

By the time the United States entered World War II, Patton, like General Douglas MacArthur, had a reputation as a flashy dresser. He wore green trousers with a black stripe, a tight green leather jacket, and a huge golden helmet. Usually, he carried two ivory-handled revolvers in a holster around his waist. His men nicknamed him "The Green Hornet," after the popular comic-book superhero.[7]

When he took over the Second Corps for the invasion of North Africa, he was appalled by the sloppy dress of its soldiers. Despite the desert heat, he ordered them to wear neckties and helmets at all times. "Each time a soldier knotted a necktie . . . and buckled on his steel helmet," the general wrote later, "he was forcibly reminded that Patton had come to command the Second Corps . . . and with that a tough new era had begun."[8]

Until Patton's arrival, Field Marshal Erwin Rommel, the "Desert Fox," had fought off the Allies in Africa. The American general was anxious to land his tanks and men. "We shall attack and attack until we are exhausted and then we shall attack again!" he told them.[9]

The Second Corps under Patton had three goals: "First to capture a beachhead, second to capture the city of Casablanca, third to move against the German wherever he may be and destroy him."[10] Within a few months, his soldiers had accomplished all three. At the Battle of El Guettar in March 1943, as commander of the Second Corps, Patton decimated Rommel's troops.

Patton was then named commander of the Seventh Army for the invasion of Sicily. It took just three weeks for the Allies to crush enemy resistance and take control of the island.

Of course, the general continued to push his men hard. He slapped two patients in military hospitals who were apparently suffering from battle fatigue. "You're a disgrace to the Army," he yelled at one of them. "You ought to be lined up against a wall and shot. In fact, I ought to shoot you myself right now."[11] Then he waved one of his pistols in the man's face.

General Dwight D. Eisenhower, Patton's superior, was not pleased. "I will not tolerate conduct of the sort described . . . by anyone, no matter how high his rank," he said.[12] Patton was ordered to apologize to his troops for the slapping incident, then he was relieved of his command.

Within a few weeks, however, he was in England, helping to plan the D-day invasion of occupied France. Eisenhower decided Patton had been punished enough; besides, the feisty general would

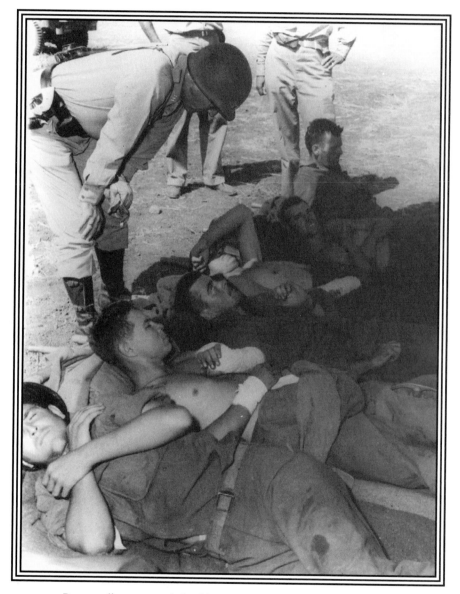

Patton talks to wounded soldiers in Sicily, Italy, on July 25, 1943.

be needed in the invasion of France. Eisenhower gave Patton command of the Third Army.

Soon Patton's men were charging across France into Germany. Along the way, he surprised—and inspired—them with his philosophy of war: "I hear a lot of crap about what a glorious thing it is to die for your country. It isn't glorious, it's stupid! You don't go into battle to die for your country, you go into battle to make [the enemy] die for *his* country."

Fighting against the Axis nations was not a complicated proposition for the general. "War is a killing business. You've got to spill their blood. Rip 'em up the belly or shoot 'em in the guts."[13]

In the last eleven months of the war in Europe, Patton's Third Army killed 144,500 enemy soldiers and wounded 366,000. They had taken 956,000 prisoners and captured 6,484 square miles of German territory. "History records no greater achievement in such a limited time," he told his troops.[14] In American history, no other general has ever covered more ground or taken more prisoners.

Eisenhower recognized that Patton's tactics had worked: "The more he drives his men the more he will save lives and the men in the Third Army know this to be true."[15] While inflicting incredible losses on the enemy, the Third Army came through with 21,441 killed, 16,200 missing, and 99,224 wounded.

When Germany surrendered, Patton was made military governor of the captured territory. He was criticized for putting former Nazis in positions of power and responsibility. Instead of worrying about their former German enemies, he suggested Americans should be more concerned with the communist U.S.S.R., which had conquered the eastern half of Germany. Even though the United States and the U.S.S.R. had been allies, he felt that they would soon be enemies. "If it's necessary to fight the Russians, the sooner we do it the better," he said. [16]

Once again, the resulting uproar over Patton's remarks caused Eisenhower to relieve him of command in October 1945. He was transferred from the command of the Third Army to that of the Fifteenth Army. On December 21, 1945, he was killed in a car accident in Heidelberg, Germany. The publication of his memoirs, *War As I Knew It,* occurred two years later.

"A leader—military or civilian—must be judged by results," said General Omar N. Bradley. "Patton . . . had a battle sense . . . which enabled him to foresee situations that were developing and make dispositions to meet them. . . . General Patton was a great leader in battle." [17]

Patton was proud of the role he played in World War II. As he told his men, "When your grandchildren ask you what you did in the war, you can tell them, 'I fought with Patton.'" [18]

8

Matthew B. Ridgway
(1895–1993)

Matthew Bunker Ridgway was born on March 3, 1895, in Fort Monroe, Virginia. When he was a little boy, he got his first rifle, an air gun, when he lived on an Army post at Walla Walla, Washington. With the rifle, he could pretend to be just like his father, Thomas, a career soldier.

When he ran out of BBs, Matthew stuffed dry winter wheat up the barrel. When he ran out of targets, he spotted a farmer bending over his tomatoes. The little boy shot him in the backside.

"It was the last time I ever pointed a weapon at man or beast without fully intending to kill, a principle pounded into my head, through the seat of my pants," Ridgway remembered.[1]

General Matthew B. Ridgway

After he graduated from West Point in 1917 and served with the Army in places like China, Nicaragua, Panama, and the Philippines, Ridgway began working with weapons much more deadly than air guns. During World War II, he was one of the first generals to lead airborne soldiers, or paratroopers. By then planes were large enough to hold groups of men, who parachuted out of them carrying supplies and weapons on their backs. They were usually dropped behind enemy lines as part of a large-scale assault. The Germans were the first to successfully use paratroopers when they took the Netherlands in 1940 and Crete in 1941.

Paratroopers also became an important part of American strategy in World War II. As commander of the 82nd Airborne Division, Ridgway pushed his men hard. His philosophy was, "Be aggressive and then more aggressive."[2]

During various campaigns in the war, Ridgway's troops landed in the Netherlands, France, Italy, and Germany. Most of the time, the general was right in the middle of the action. "The place of a commander is where he anticipates the crisis of action is going to be."[3] On D-day he was dropped behind the German lines with his men:

> Wing to wing, the big planes snuggled close in their tight formation, we crossed to the coast of France. I was sitting straight across the aisle from the doorless exit . . . No light showed on the land, but in the pale glow of a rising moon, I could

clearly see each farm and field below. And I remember thinking how peaceful the land looked . . . . The jump master, crouched in the door, went out with a yell—"Let's go!" With a paratrooper . . . breathing hard on my neck, I leaped out after him.[4]

As soon as he landed, Ridgway thought he saw something moving in the darkness. Was it American—or German? "Flash!" he yelled, waiting to hear the agreed upon response "Thunder." But there was no answer and he prepared to fire his pistol. Suddenly he realized he was staring at a cow. "I could have kissed her."[5] If there was a cow in the field, the area must be clear of mines. For a few moments at least, he and his men would be safe.

However, they soon were under heavy German fire. Ridgway's troops had orders to advance through a crossing but, frightened by the noise, explosion, and death all around them, they were turning around and running back. "I jumped up and ran down there," he said. "We grabbed these men, turned them around, pushed, shoved, even led them by hand until we got them started across."[6]

During intense action, many of his men fell, but the crossing was cleared of German soldiers and opened for the advancing Americans. Another commander said he had never seen so many dead Germans. Ridgway said proudly, "I think that fight was as hot a single battle as any U.S. troops had, at any time, during the war in Europe."[7]

Within three months, the Allies had pushed most of the Germans out of France. That set the stage for Operation Market-Garden, a daring plan to land British and American troops in the Netherlands, opening the way into Germany itself.

By then, Ridgway commanded the XVIII Corps. On the third day of the offensive, despite heavy German artillery fire, he parachuted into Holland to join his men. "The whole world exploded," he said. "A German bomber formation . . . was tearing that town apart. . . . Great fires were burning everywhere, ammo trucks were exploding, gasoline trucks were on fire, and debris from wrecked houses clogged the streets."[8]

The general was not the only one who ran into problems. Operation Market-Garden was a disaster. When many of the paratroopers got too far ahead of the ground troops, the Germans held their ground. This resulted in many casualties.

Encouraged by their success in the Netherlands, the Germans stunned the Allies with the daring Ardennes Offensive in December 1944. The advance punched a huge bulge in the Allied lines. Adolf Hitler's troops seemed to be close to breaking through. The Americans and British were forced to retreat in what became known as the Battle of the Bulge. Part of the reason for the plan's success was the German use of paratroopers, disguised as Americans, who landed behind Allied lines.

Ridgway's men were part of the effort that finally stopped the German advance. During heavy fighting, he was alone when he heard a loud noise and then saw a German armored, self-propelled gun coming at him. Luckily he was carrying his old Springfield rifle with armor-piercing cartridges. "I swung around, firing my Springfield, and I got five shots in fast, at the swastika." The machine went a few more feet, then rumbled to a stop.[9]

Most of Ridgway's troops fought gallantly, but there were some exceptions. During the Battle of the Bulge, the general saw a lieutenant leading a dozen men away from the fighting. The German machine-gun fire, he explained, had been too much for them. "I relieved him of his command there on the spot. I told him that he was a disgrace to his country and his uniform and that I was ashamed of him, and I knew the members of his patrol were equally ashamed."[10] Ridgway turned command of the patrol over to a sergeant who turned the men around and headed back into battle.

On March 24, 1944, American and British paratroopers dropped on the eastern side of the Rhine River in Germany itself. It was a dangerous operation; twenty-two of the seventy-two C-46 planes were downed by enemy ground fire. Many of them simply exploded as soon as they were hit. The general called the C-46 "a fire trap" and said his men would never jump from them again.

Ridgway's paratroopers, along with the British, landed in Germany. Here, after the war, Ridgway (right) greets British Field Marshal Bernard Montgomery (left).

They didn't have to. The drop across the Rhine was the last major airborne operation of World War II. Ridgway himself crossed into Germany in an amphibious vehicle a few days later. Shortly after he switched to a jeep, the general spotted German soldiers running nearby. He jumped out of the vehicle and began firing the Springfield. When he exhausted his ammunition he ducked behind the jeep to load another clip. There was a loud blast as a German grenade exploded just two feet from his head. Fortunately one of the tires was between him and the blast. He received just a minor wound in his shoulder. When his small group had cleared out the enemy, his only comment was, "I think I got one of them." He did not bother to mention that he had been injured.[11]

In the closing days of the war in Europe, the Allies surrounded the huge German army, commanded by Field Marshal Walther Model. The situation was hopeless for the Germans. Ridgway wanted to win the war quickly, but he saw no reason to needlessly slaughter a beaten army.

The general sent a messenger to Model, reminding him of the great American General Robert E. Lee, who fought bravely in the Civil War, but surrendered when his cause became hopeless. "The same choice is now yours," he wrote. "For the sake of your nation's future, lay down your arms at once. The German lives you will save are sorely needed to restore your people to their proper place in society."[12]

Model refused Ridgway's kind message. The field marshal had already promised Adolf Hitler, the German leader, that he would never surrender. The fighting and dying continued for two more weeks.

After the war, Ridgway became commander of the Mediterranean theater, and then the Caribbean command. In 1949 he was appointed Army Deputy Chief of Staff before taking command of the Eighth Army in Korea a year later. In 1952 Ridgway became Supreme Commander of American troops in Europe.

In Korea, Ridgway again proved to be an effective leader. In 1950 he helped drive the Chinese out of South Korea. The next year, he was promoted to overall Allied commander in the Far East where he continued to defend South Korea from Chinese troops. At this post he also helped rebuild war-torn Japan.

After his service in Korea, Ridgway became Supreme Allied Commander in Europe and was then appointed Army Chief of Staff in 1953. He retired in 1955, publishing his memoirs, *Soldier,* a year later. Matthew Bunker Ridgway was ninety-eight when he died on July 26, 1993.

At the end of World War II, General George C. Marshall had high praise for his friend:

General Ridgway has firmly established himself in history as a great battle leader. The advance of his Army Corps . . . in the last phase of the war in Europe was sensational. . . . His campaign in Korea will be rated as a classic of personal leadership. As Supreme Commander of the North Atlantic Treaty Organization (NATO) in Europe, he did a splendid job.[13]

9

Holland M. Smith

(1882–1967)

Holland McTyeire Smith was born on April 20, 1882, in Seale, Alabama. When Smith was growing up in Alabama, his father, John V. Smith, was a lawyer. Holland decided he wanted to follow the same profession, so he earned a law degree from the University of Alabama.

However, two years as a lawyer were enough to convince Holland that he should choose a different profession. He decided he wanted a new career as an officer in the Army. But when he got to Washington, D.C., he was told that the Marine Corps was the only branch of service accepting new officers.

"What are the Marines?" he asked.[1] It was explained that a Marine is a soldier who serves at sea, then moves to the land to fight. Despite Smith's

General Holland M. Smith

ignorance, the United States Marine Corps had been an important part of America's defenses since 1775.

Smith joined the Corps in 1905 and loved the Marines for the rest of his life. He always felt that the Navy and the Army got most of the attention and the supplies. "After the feast," he wrote, "the crumbs were given to the Marines—if there were any crumbs."[2]

Smith's first assignment was in the Philippines. Even though he liked to be called "Hoke" by his friends, in the islands he picked up the nickname "Howlin' Mad." He had little patience, and when it ran out, he let people know, loudly and clearly.

After serving in Panama and Santo Domingo, he saw battle action in France during World War I. Then he was stationed in Haiti and with the Pacific Fleet. Later he joined the headquarters staff in Washington, D.C., where he helped prepare the Marines for World War II.

Smith knew that the Marines would need new landing boats. He helped design fast, shallow launches that could carry men and vehicles to beaches.

In 1940 he took the First Marine Brigade to Cuba for six months of vigorous training. Working twelve hours a day, seven days a week, they first cleared five hundred acres of swamp, then built their own living quarters. After that, they practiced amphibious landings, in which they raced off the landing craft and seized imaginary enemy strongholds. Working with his men, Smith helped develop combat techniques that would soon be put to the test.

Shortly after the attack on Pearl Harbor, Smith turned sixty years old. Despite his age and problems with diabetes, a kidney disease, he asked to be assigned to a combat unit. It took an order from President Franklin D. Roosevelt to grant his wish. Soon Smith was assigned again to the Pacific Fleet. The president wanted him there to help lead the men who would be storming the Japanese atolls, or islands, between Hawaii and Japan. There the general would earn at least two new nicknames—"the Pacific Cyclone" and "Old Man of the Atolls."

Using the amphibious techniques Smith had helped develop, Marines took Guadalcanal from the Japanese in February 1943 after a six-month battle. Some of the soldiers called it "Operation Shoestring" because most of the Allies' efforts were concentrated on Europe and the fight against Germany and Italy. The Japanese did not notice that the Marines were short on soldiers or supplies; they called Guadalcanal the "Island of Death."[3]

Smith was in charge of the Marines who landed on Tarawa in November 1943. "No sooner had we hit the water than the Japanese machine guns really opened up on us," wrote Robert Sherrod, a *Time* magazine correspondent. "It was painfully slow, wading in such deep water. . . . I was scared as I had never been scared before. Those who were not hit would always remember how the machine gun bullets hissed into the water, inches to the right, inches to the left."[4]

The Japanese defenders were confident that they could stop the Americans. "A million men cannot take Tarawa in a hundred years," said Rear Admiral Keiji Shibasaki.

But once on the beach, the Marines who had survived used tanks, rifles, and flamethrowers to rout the enemy in just four days. More than a thousand Americans and forty-eight hundred Japanese were killed in what would prove to be one of the bloodiest battles of the war.

Some Americans wondered if the cost for taking the tiny island of Tarawa had been too high. Smith had little patience with their complaints: "We've got the toughest and smartest fighting men in the world. But as long as the war lasts some of them somewhere will be getting killed. We have got to acknowledge that or else we might as well stay home."[5]

The general pointed out that the Americans had learned valuable lessons from the short, bloody battle. From then on, before they assaulted a beach, underwater demolition teams would clear the way. "It took Europe nineteen years to learn how to fight Napoleon . . . It took the Marines just three days to learn how to storm an atoll fortress and dig the Japs out."[6]

The attack on Makin a few days later went much more smoothly. "There is nothing more beautiful in war than an amphibious operation when it clicks," wrote an historian, "and this one did." Just sixty-six Americans died in this operation.

Next the Marines attacked the Mariana Islands: Guam, Saipan, and Tinian. As soon as the Americans landed on the beach, the Japanese soldiers charged, waving sabers and shooting rifles. "When they hit us there were so many of them we couldn't shoot fast enough," remembered Technical Sergeant Frederick Stiltz. "We must have killed 300 or 400 Japs; they were piled around us."[7]

The other islands were just as tough. "I landed on Guam with the third wave to find the beaches literally covered with dead Marines," said Louis Webb. "Just about every palm tree had its top blown off. Blood and carnage was everywhere."[8]

But by August 15, 1944, the Marianas belonged to the Americans. Soon Tinian, one of the Mariana islands, was turned into the largest air base in the world for the B-29 bombers, which would be raining destruction on Japan itself.

The bloodiest battle of the Pacific would be fought on Iwo Jima. This island covered just eight square miles and was called "probably the world's most heavily defended island."[9]

"It's a tough proposition," said Smith before the battle. "That's why my Marines are here . . . Every man, every cook, baker, and candlestick maker will be down on the beaches, somewhere with some kind of weapons."[10]

Smith (right) takes a jeep tour of an airfield on the Mariana Island of Saipan. Tinian, another one of the Mariana Islands, was converted into the largest air base in the world for B-29 bombers.

For eighty minutes early in the morning of February 19, 1945, American guns poured fire on the beaches of Iwo Jima. It was an awesome spectacle. "Maybe the [island] will blow up and sink into the ocean and then we can all go home," one man joked.[11] Then 485 ships landed Smith's Marines.

The general had been right; the Japanese defended the island furiously. "The first night on Iwo Jima can only be described as a nightmare in hell," wrote correspondent Sherrod.

> About the beach in the morning lay the dead. They had died with the greatest possible violence. Nowhere in the Pacific have I seen such badly mangled bodies. Many were cut squarely in half. Legs and arms lay fifty feet from any body.[12]

Smith landed briefly on the beaches, before he was ordered off by Admiral Chester W. Nimitz. A reporter said he was hard to miss—"clad in a spotted jumper, grasping a carbine, jumping up and down, alternately swearing and beaming over his spectacles."[13] Before Smith returned to his ship, a sniper's bullet narrowly missed him.

Even before the battle ended on March 26, 1945, B-29 bombers were taking off from Iwo Jimo. More than five thousand Marines died there. A survivor called the battle "as horrible as any action in Marine Corps history . . . if you were going to survive, you just had to be lucky, that's all."[14]

Five months later Japan surrendered in a ceremony aboard the U.S.S. *Missouri* in Tokyo Bay, but

Nimitz did not allow Smith to attend. The general was the highest-ranking officer in the Pacific not invited. Once again, as Smith liked to point out, "the crumbs" were for the Marines. He and his men never seemed to get the recognition they had earned.

But nobody could argue with what Lieutenant General Holland M. Smith's Marines had accomplished. From Guadalcanal all the way to Okinawa, they had pushed the Japanese ten thousand miles back toward their homeland.

Smith retired in 1946 and lived quietly until his death on January 1, 1967. As a general, he never had any doubts about the capabilities of his Marines. After Iwo Jima, Smith told a friend, "I was not afraid of the outcome of the battle. I knew we would win. We always did."[15]

General Joseph W. Stilwell

Joseph W. Stilwell

(1883–1946)

Born on March 19, 1883, in Palatka, Florida, Joseph Warren Stilwell grew to know more about China than anyone else in the United States Army. Two decades before World War II, he spent four years studying Chinese art, literature, and language, as well as its military history. Years later his two daughters acquired similar interests. One was a musician who performed Chinese music; the other was a painter who imitated the style of Chinese artists.

But Stilwell also admired the Chinese military. After graduating from West Point Military Academy in 1904, he served in Tienstin, China from 1926 to 1929 and was a military attaché in Peking from 1935 to 1939. After spending these years stationed in

China, Stilwell said, "The Chinese soldier is one of the best in the world. If he has the equipment and supplies, no one can lick him."[1]

Nine days after the attack on Pearl Harbor, Japanese forces invaded Burma. The small Asian country was a British colony located between India and China. The Japanese hoped to gain control of Burma so that they could cut off the flow of supplies from the British in India to the forces of Generalissimo Chiang Kai-shek in China.

Chiang was an ally of the United States and Great Britain, but he had more to worry about than just the Japanese threat to his nation. His rule was being threatened by Mao Zedong and the Chinese Communists, who wanted to take over their country from Chiang and the Nationalists.

Supplies from the Allies made their way to Chiang from Rangoon along the Burma Road. It was this link the Japanese hoped to cut. The small Burmese army was unable to slow the invaders.

Stilwell was sent back by his American commanders to take charge of Chinese troops early in 1942. By then, the situation was hopeless. The Japanese had taken just five months to conquer Burma.

Stilwell, a quarrelsome man who wasn't afraid to state his opinions, was nicknamed "Vinegar Joe" for his sour disposition. His description of the Allied defeat was terse: "The Japs ran us out of Burma. We took a beating!"[2] He did not enjoy losing. "It is humiliating . . . I think we ought to find out what caused it, go back and retake it."[3]

But before he and the Allies could come up with a strategy to retake Burma, they had to escape the victorious Japanese by fleeing to China or India. Lieutenant General William Slim led the British troops on a long, slow, hot retreat through central Burma into India. Throughout the march, he encouraged his men and won their respect and affection. They called him "Uncle Bill."

Stilwell was not pleased by Slim's strategy. He thought the British had retreated so quickly that his troops were left virtually alone to face the invaders. He had to retreat 150 grueling miles through the jungle with a small band of troops and a few Burmese nurses.

The American general wasn't known for his personal warmth. He didn't spend his time encouraging his men or trying to boost their spirits; he concentrated on keeping them moving. Almost immediately, they had to give up their trucks and jeeps; the jungle trails were too narrow for them. There was no way to escape except on foot.

"We will all stay together in one group," he told them. "But I insist on discipline. If anyone does not want to accept my orders without question, he'd better speak up right now—and go his own way."[4] Nobody spoke up.

They marched fifty minutes, rested ten, then got up and marched again. Many times the jungle trails disappeared entirely and it was impossible even to walk through the thick growth. Stilwell led his men down to the Chaunggyi River, where they splashed ahead until finding another opening in the jungle.

Despite the rough terrain and the heat, Stilwell's troops were able to average about fifteen miles a day. After seventeen days, they finally reached the safety of Imphal, India. The general said he would never forget the march. "I'm keeping it right in my mind until the day we march into Tokyo."[5]

With no more land link to China, the Allies had to supply the Chinese leader Chiang Kai-Shek from the air. Thousands of planes made the dangerous flight from Assam, India, to China. Several thousand Chinese troops were flown to India to join what was left of Stilwell's forces. He and the British generals began formulating strategy to reopen the Burma Road.

Some Allied leaders felt it would be foolish to try to fight the Japanese on the ground. Why not just try to bomb them out of Burma? Winston Churchill said, "Going into the swampy jungles to fight the Japanese is like going into the water to fight a shark."[6] Stilwell disagreed: "It's the ground soldier slogging through the mud and fighting in the trenches who will win the war."[7]

Stilwell got his way and was allowed to approve an incredibly ambitious plan to construct a 478-mile road through rugged mountains from Ledo, India, to Myitkyina, Burma. There it would join the Burma

Road and once again there would be a pathway for troops and supplies into China. It would be tough enough to build such a road in peacetime, but construction, of course, could not begin until Allied troops had taken the land back from the Japanese.

At first Stilwell's Chinese troops fought poorly. Chiang had ordered them to go slowly because he wanted them to be fresh in case he needed them to fight against the Chinese Communists. Stilwell was furious. Why, he wondered, were we bothering to supply the Chinese Nationalists when they would not wage all-out war against the Japanese?

But progress was made because of two tough, relatively small Allied units. General Orde Wingate commanded three thousand British soldiers known as "Chindits," named after the Burmese word for lion. They slipped through the thick jungle in small groups to torment the Japanese. They carried few supplies, usually not even a shaving kit so many of them wore beards. Because of their light loads and small groups, they were able to move quickly and stealthily, doing much of their work behind enemy lines.

On the American side, General Frank Merrill commanded a similar group of guerrilla fighters known as Merrill's Marauders. Throughout much of the action, they were assisted by the Kachins, a tribe of Burmese who knew the jungle well.

The Americans finally had to blackmail the Chinese into fighting harder. Chiang was told that unless his troops began waging serious war against the Japanese, the Allies would withhold the supplies that he needed.

In May 1944 the combined Allied forces began closing in on Myitkyina. Much of the heavy fighting was done by British troops. Stilwell, of course, continued to push the men hard who were under his command. Carrying a rifle and ignoring enemy bullets, he sometimes traveled to the front himself. If he wanted his men to be tough, he figured he had to show them that he was tough, too.

After the death of Wingate, their commander, Stilwell turned the exhausted Chindits from guerrilla fighters into assault soldiers. They did poorly and took many casualties. At Myitkyina, he did the same thing with Merrill's Mauraders. Soldiers who had been marching and fighting almost continuously for six months were thrown against the entrenched Japanese forces. Other troops had to be brought in, and it wasn't until the enemy's supply lines were cut from behind that Myitkyina finally fell.

As soon as the town was taken, construction began on a pipeline that would bring fuel from Ledo. The Myitkyina airfield could then be used for supply flights into China. It was a much safer, more direct route than the ones that had been used since the fall of Burma.

Right behind the soldiers came the engineers and workers whose job it was to construct the Ledo road over the newly captured territory. Much of the work

Stilwell enters his cottage in Kunming, China, in 1944.

had to be done during the monsoon season, when heavy rains drenched the country. The Americans did not let the thick jungle, the continuing floods, or jungle diseases stop them. When faced by almost two miles of flooded roadbed, the crews used a million board feet of lumber to build a causeway over the water. Late in 1943, 80 percent of the workers were suffering from malaria. But the work continued because, as General T. F. Farrell explained, "General Stilwell was depending upon the road to supply his winter campaign against the Japanese."[8] Even when cutting through rugged mountain terrain, the engineers were able to build a mile of road a day.

As the Allies continued to slowly chase the Japanese out of Burma, Stilwell was increasingly frustrated by his dealings with Chiang. The Chinese leader, he felt, was not interested enough in defeating the Japanese. The Nationalists seemed to be more interested in getting rich and fighting the Chinese Communists. Stilwell complained that much of the aid money pouring into China was going into the pockets of Chiang and his generals and not into buying supplies for their army. Chiang grew tired of listening to Stilwell's complaints.

The fighting went on, and the road was eventually completed. It was first named the Ledo Road but was renamed after Stilwell in early 1945. By May the Japanese had been forced out of Burma. The next month, Stilwell took command of the United States Tenth Army of the Pacific and saw one hundred thousand Japanese troops surrender at Ryukyu Islands in August.

After the war Stilwell was stationed in San Francisco as Sixth Army commander where he died on October 12, 1946.

Stilwell helped the Allies win the biggest war in the history of the world, but it was not a job he enjoyed. "War is the most wasteful and immoral device ever contrived by man. . . . It's always bound to be a dirty game, and it is bound to be played by dirty rules. . . . But whatever happens . . . we've got to win, no matter what the rules."[9]

Chapter Notes

Chapter 1. Henry H. Arnold

1. Editors of Army Times, *Famous American Military Leaders of World War II* (New York: Dodd, Mead & Company, 1962), p. 94.

2. Robert Leckie, *The Story of World War II* (New York: Random House, 1964), p. 136.

3. C.L. Sulzberger, *The American Heritage Picture History of World War II* (New York: Crown Publishers, 1966), p. 420.

4. Ibid.

Chapter 2. Omar N. Bradley

1. Omar N. Bradley, *A Soldier's Story* (New York: Henry Holt and Company, 1951), pp. 29–30.

2. Relman Morin, *Dwight D. Eisenhower: A Gauge of Greatness* (New York: Associated Press, 1969), p. 26.

3. Bradley, p. 59.

4. Ibid., p. 85.

5. Michael Wright, ed. *The World at Arms* (London: Reader's Digest Association, 1989), p. 303.

6. Ibid., p. 310.

7. John Toland, *The Last 100 Days* (New York: Random House, 1965), p. 216.

8. Wright, p. 312.

Chapter 3. Dwight D. Eisenhower

1. Merle Miller, *Ike the Soldier* (New York: G. P. Putnam's Sons, 1987), pp.102–103.

2. Relman Morin, *Dwight D. Eisenhower: A Gauge of Greatness* (New York: Associated Press, 1969), p. 26.

3. William F. Longgood, Ike: *A Pictorial Biography* (New York: Time–Life Books, 1969), p. 29.

4. Morin, p. 56.

5. Ibid.

6. Ibid., p. 67.

7. Ibid., p. 88.

8. Ibid., p. 97.

9. Russ Weigley, *Eisenhower's Lieutenants: The Campaign of France & Germany, 1944–1945* (Bloomington: Indiana University Press, 1981), p. 75.

10. Ibid., p. 66.

11. Morin, p. 107.

12. Ibid, p. 124.

13. Longgood, p. 77.

Chapter 4. Curtis E. LeMay

1. General Curtis E. LeMay with MacKinlay Kantor, *Mission With LeMay: My Story* (New York: Doubleday & Company, 1965), pp.13–14.

2. Thomas M. Coffey, *Iron Eagle: The Turbulent Life of General Curtis E. LeMay* (New York: Crown Publishers, 1986), p. 87.

3. Ibid., pp. 95–96.

4. LeMay, p. 384.

5. Coffey, p. 161.

6. LeMay, p. 375.

7. Ibid.

8. Michael Wright, ed. *The World at Arms* (London: Reader's Digest Association Limited, 1989), p. 437.

9. Coffey, p. 59.

Chapter 5. Douglas MacArthur

1. William Manchester, *American Caesar* (Boston: (Little, Brown and Company, 1978), p. 88.

2. Douglas MacArthur, *Duty Honor Country: MacArthur: A Pictorial Autobiography* (New York: Time, Incorporated, 1965), p. 23.

3. Manchester, p. 85.

4. MacArthur, p. 53.

5. Michael Wright, ed. *The World at Arms* (London: Reader's Digest Association, Limited, 1989), p. 146.

6. MacArthur, pp. 60–61.

7. Ibid., p. 61.

8. Manchester, p. 250.

9. MacArthur, p. 71.

10. Editors of *Army Times, Famous American Military Leaders of World War II* (New York: Dodd, Mead & Company, 1962), p. 38.

11. MacArthur, p. 96.

12. Ibid., p. 117.

13. Merle Miller, *Plain Speaking: An Oral Biography of Harry S Truman* (New York: Berkley, 1973), p. 294.

14. James B. Sweeney, *Army Leaders of World War II* (New York: Franklin Watts, 1984), p. 46.

15. MacArthur, p. 198.

Chapter 6. George C. Marshall

1. David McCullough, *Truman* (New York: Simon & Schuster, 1992), p. 534.

2. Bob Frost, "The Man Who Saved the World . . . Twice," *Biography*, vol. 1, no. 8, August 1997, p. 87.

3. Editors of *Army Times*, *Famous American Military Leaders of World War II* (New York: Dodd, Mead & Company, 1962), p. 16.

4. Ibid., p. 18.

5. Robert Leckie, *The Story of World War II* (New York: Random House, 1964), p. 92.

6. Ibid., p. 100.

7. Ed Cray, *General of the Army: George C. Marshall, Soldier and Statesman* (New York: W. W. Norton & Company, 1990), p. 13.

8. Ibid., p. 531.

9. *Think Magazine's Diary of U. S. Participation in World War II* (New York: International Business Machines Corporation, 1946), p. 337.

10. Merle Miller, *Plain Speaking: An Oral Biography of Harry S Truman* (New York: Berkley, 1973), p. 233.

11. Forest C. Pogue, *George C. Marshall: Ordeal and Hope: 1939–1942* (New York: Viking, 1966), p. 11.

12. Miller, p. 234.

13. McCullough, p. 614.

Chapter 7. George S. Patton

1. Ian V. Hogg, *The Biography of General George S. Patton* (New York: Galley Press, 1982), p. 45.

2. Editors of *Army Times*, *Famous Military Leaders of World War II* (New York: Dodd, Mead & Company, 1962), p. 73.

3. James B. Sweeney, *Army Leaders of World War II* (New York: Franklin Watts, 1984), p. 68.

4. Hogg, p. 13.

5. Martin Blumenson, *Patton: The Man Behind the Legend* (New York: William Morrow and Company, 1985), p. 113.

6. Ibid., p. 114.

7. Hogg, pp. 34–35.

8. Sweeney, p. 75.

9. *Army Times*, p. 69.

10. Hogg, p. 45.

11. Ibid., p. 76.

12. Ibid., p. 78.

13. Ibid., p. 35.

14. Ibid., p. 147

15. George Forty, *Patton's Third Army at War* (New York: Charles Scribner's Sons, 1978), p. 57.

16. Sweeney, p. 77.

17. Forty, p. 64.

18. Hogg, p. 153.

Chapter 8. Matthew B. Ridgway

1. General Matthew B. Ridgway, *Soldier: The Memoirs of Matthew B. Ridgway as told to Harold H. Martin* (New York: Harper & Brothers, 1956), p. 23.

2. John Toland, *The Last 100 Days* (New York: Random House, 1965), p. 282.

3. Ridgway, p. 13.

4. C.L. Sulzberger, *The American Heritage Picture History of World War II* (New York: Crown Publishers, 1966), p. 502.

5. Ridgway, pp. 5–6.

6. Ibid., p. 14.

7. Ibid.

8. Ibid., p. 110.

9. Ibid., p. 116.

10. Ibid., p. 121.

11. Toland, p. 283.

12. Ibid., p. 391.

13. Ridgway, forward.

Chapter 9. Holland M. Smith

1. Anna Rothe, ed. *Current Biography* (New York: H. W. Wilson Company, 1945), p. 557.

2. General Holland M. Smith and Percy Finch, "My Troubles With the Army on Saipan," *Saturday Evening Post,* November 13, 1949.

3. Editors of VFW Magazine, *Faces of Victory: Pacific: The Fall of the Rising Sun* (Kansas City: Addax Publishing Group, 1995), p. 69.

4. Ibid., p. 124.

5. Rothe, p. 558.

6. Ibid.

7. VFW Magazine, p. 133.

8. Ibid, p. 135.

9. Rothe, p. 558.

10. Bill D. Ross, *Iwo Jima: Legacy of Valor* (New York: Vanguard Press, 1985), p. 46.

11. Ibid., p. 60.

12. Ibid., p. 80.

13. Rothe, p. 558.

14. VFW Magazine, p. 146.

15. Ross, p. 47.

Chapter 10. Joseph W. Stilwell

1. 1942 Current Biography, p. 808.

2. Robert Leckie, *The Story of World War II* (New York: Random House, 1964), pp. 88–89.

3. Michael Wright, ed. *The World at Arms* (London: Reader's Digest Association, 1989), p. 155.

4. Frank Dorn, *Walkout with Stilwell in Burma* (New York: Thomas Y. Crowell Company, 1971), p. 153.

5. Ibid., p. 211.

6. C. L. Sulzberger, *The American Heritage Picture History of World War II* (New York: Crown Publishers, 1966), p. 331.

7. Ibid.

8. *Think Magazine's Diary of U. S. Participation in World War II* (New York: International Business Machines Corporation, 1946), p. 355.

9. Dorn, p. 147.

Further Reading

Arnold, Henry H. *Global Mission.* North Stratford, N.H.: Ayer Company Publishers, Inc., 1972.

Brown, Clayton. *Dwight D. Eisenhower.* Springfield, N.J.: Enslow Publishers, Inc., 1998.

Darby, Jean. *Douglas MacArthur.* Minneapolis: The Lerner Group, 1989.

Eisenhower, Dwight D. *Crusade In Europe.* New York: Doubleday & Company, Inc., 1990.

————. *Dear General: Eisenhower's Wartime Letters to Marshall.* Ann Arbor: Books on Demand, reprint (date not supplied).

Finke, Blythe F. *General Patton: Fearless Military Leader.* Charlotteville, N.Y.: SamHar Press, 1972.

Finkelstein, Norman. *Douglas MacArthur: The Emperor General: A Biography of Douglas MacArthur.* Parsippany, N.J.: Silver Burdett Press, 1989.

Hudson, Wilma J. *Dwight D. Eisenhower: Young Military Leader.* Old Tappan, N.J.: Simon and Schuster Children's, 1992.

MacArthur, Douglas. *Reminiscences.* New York: Da Capo Press, Inc., 1985.

Marshall, George C. *General Marshall's Victory Report on the Winning of World War II in Europe & the Pacific.* Tigerton, Wis.: Aelred A. Meverden Publisher, 1989.

Patton Jr., George S. *War As I Knew It.* Boston: Houghton Mifflin Company, 1978.

Peifer Jr., Charles. *George Patton: Soldier of Destiny: A Biography of George Patton.* Parsippany, N.J.: Silver Burdett Press, 1988.

Ridgway, Matthew B. *The Korean War.* New York: Da Capo Press, Inc., 1986.

Saunders, Alan. *George C. Marshall.* New York: Facts on File, Inc., 1995.

Smith, Holland M. *Coral and Brass.* Washington D.C.: Zenger Publishing Company, Inc., 1981.

Stein, R. Conrad. *World War II in Europe: "America Goes to War."* Hillside, N.J.: Enslow Publishers, Inc., 1994.

———. *World War II in the Pacific: "Remember Pearl Harbor."* Hillside, N.J.: Enslow Publishers, Inc., 1994.

Index